THIS FAST I CHOOSE

A DAYBOOK FOR LENT

Friendship Press • New York

© 1990 by Friendship Press
Editorial Offices:
475 Riverside Drive, Room 772, New York, NY 10115
Distribution Offices:
P.O. Box 37844, Cincinnati, OH 45222-0844

Manufactured in the United States of America
94 93 92 91 90   5 4 3 2 1

Library of Congress Cataloging-in-Publication Data

This fast I choose : a daybook for Lent.
        p.   cm.
    ISBN 0-377-00201-1
    1. Lent—Prayer-books and devotions—English.
BV85.T425   1990
242'.34–dc20   89-28338
                                CIP

PREFACE

This Fast I Choose: A Daybook for Lent presents carefully chosen Bible passages for each day of Lent — in the New Revised Standard Version translation.

Taking its cue from Isaiah 58:6–9, the selections and accompanying texts are designed to lead the reader to a response that helps to heal the wounds of our modern world, fulfilling the prophet's exhortation to...

> ...loose the bonds of injustice,
> ...share your bread with the hungry,
> ...when you see the naked cover them,
> ...satisfy the needs of the afflicted.
> Then you shall call and the Lord will answer.

The NewRSV translation used in the daybook is unique. Almost twenty years in the making, no other Bible has been prepared by an ecumenical committee of men and women who represent not only a variety of Protestant traditions but also Roman Catholic, Eastern Orthodox, and Jewish communities. Under the direction of Dr. Bruce M. Metzger, the committee was instructed to "introduce such changes as are warranted on the basis of accuracy, clarity, euphony, and current English usage." Changes include:

- Replacement of archaic words.
- Correction of confusing word order.
- Update of English words that have changed in meaning.
- Restoration of common gender words that were intended in the ancient languages.
- Replacement of masculine pronouns when both men and women are clearly intended.
- Improving the clarity for oral reading.
- Improving the sound of the text.

Brief quotations from Emily Dickinson, Julian of Norwich, Oscar Romero, Mahatma Gandhi, Nadine Gordimer, and other outstanding prophets, as well as from the Christian churches around the world have also been included in the daybook to enhance the meditation for the day.

Among the purposes of this Lenten daybook is to encourage two important spiritual disciplines: meditative reading of Scripture and reflective journal-keeping. The Scripture selections included here for Sundays and principal festivals are taken from the Common Lectionary Cycle A, based on the common text chosen by the Consultation on Ecumenical Hymnody, 1978, as it appears in the *Lutheran Book of Worship* (Minneapolis: Augsburg Publishing House, and Philadelphia: Board of Publication, Lutheran Church in America, 1978). Weekday readings are taken from the Daily Lectionary, Year Two. The verses excerpted from each of the readings were chosen because they relate to the other readings for the day. These excerpts were made after prayerful reflection, though you may choose to read the passages in their entirety.

Journal-keeping involves daily reflection on God's acts in our personal and corporate lives. To encourage you to make the book a personal Lenten journal, space is provided on each day's page for notes. Journal-keeping is another way to be open to the Spirit. It enables us literally to "take note" of our feelings, thinking, wonderings, questions, and inspirations. Doing these two activities at the same time each day — whether we feel like it or not — helps us incorporate them into our lives as spiritual disciplines.

It is our hope that the daybook will be a valued companion for you in your preparation for Easter.

The Editors of
Friendship Press

Is not this the fast that I choose:
   to loose the bonds of injustice,
   to undo the thongs of the yoke,
to let the oppressed go free,
   and to break every yoke?
Is it not to share your bread with the hungry,
   and bring the homeless poor into your house;
when you see the naked, to cover them,
   and not to hide yourself from your own kin?
Then your light shall break forth like the dawn,
   and your healing shall spring up quickly;
your vindicator shall go before you,
   the glory of the LORD shall be your rear guard.
Then you shall call, and the LORD will answer,
   ...Here I am....

                —Isaiah 58:6–9

_____

_____

_____

_____

_____

_____

_____

_____

_____

_____

First Reading: Joel 2:12–19

^{12} Yet even now, says the LORD,
   return to me with all your heart,
with fasting, with weeping, and with
      mourning;
^{13} rend your hearts and not your clothing.
Return to the LORD, your God,
   for he is gracious and merciful,
slow to anger, and abounding in steadfast
   love....

Second Reading: 2 Corinthians 5:20b–6:2

^{2} See, now is the acceptable time; see, now
is the day of salvation!

Gospel: Matthew 6:1–6, 16–21

^{16} "And whenever you fast, do not look
dismal, like the hypocrites, for they dis-
figure their faces so as to show others that
they are fasting. Truly I tell you, they have
received their reward. ^{17} But when you
fast, put oil on your head and wash your
face, ^{18} so that your fasting may be seen
not by others but by your Father who is in
secret; and your Father who sees in secret
will reward you...."

Create in me a clean heart, O God,
   and put a new and right spirit within me.
                —Psalm 51:10

THURSDAY AFTER
ASH WEDNESDAY

_____

_____

_____

First Reading:
Habakkuk 3:1–10 (11–15) 16–18

_____

_____

²O LORD, I have heard of your renown,
and I stand in awe, O LORD, of your
work.
In our own time revive it;
in our own time make it known....

_____

_____

_____

_____

Second Reading: Philippians 3:12–21

¹³ ...this one thing I do: forgetting what
lies behind and straining forward to what
lies ahead, ¹⁴ I press on toward the goal for
the prize of the heavenly call of God in
Christ Jesus.

> *...on toward the goal...*
> We will make Jesus into every-
> thing possible so as not to face
> the one thing he is — God's
> challenge and invitation. In
> every naming of Jesus there
> lurks the danger that he be-
> comes not the challenge of God
> who demands free response
> but the divine hero who rescues
> us.... Jesus, the divine hero,
> evokes our sincerest thanks;
> Jesus, the divine challenge,
> evokes responsible action in
> the world.
>
> *–John Shea*

Gospel: John 17:1–8

¹ After Jesus had spoken these words, he
looked up to heaven and said, "Father,
the hour has come; glorify your Son so
that the Son may glorify you, ² since you
have given him authority over all people,
to give eternal life to all whom you have
given him. ³ And this is eternal life, that
they may know you, the only true God,
and Jesus Christ whom you have sent.
⁴ I glorified you on earth by finishing the
work that you gave me to do...."

Have mercy on me, O God,
according to your steadfast love....
— Psalm 51:1

7

FRIDAY AFTER
ASH WEDNESDAY

First Reading: Ezekiel 18:1–4, 25–32

³¹ Cast away from you all the transgressions that you have committed against me, and get yourselves a new heart and a new spirit! Why will you die, O house of Israel? ³² For I have no pleasure in the death of anyone, says the Lord GOD. Turn, then, and live.

Second Reading: Philippians 4:1–9

⁸ Finally, beloved, whatever is true, whatever is honorable, whatever is just, whatever is pure, whatever is pleasing, whatever is commendable, if there is any excellence, and if there is anything worthy of praise, think about these things.

Gospel: John 17:9–19

¹⁵ I am not asking you to take them out of the world, but I ask you to protect them from the evil one. ¹⁶ They do not belong to the world, just as I do not belong to the world. ¹⁷ Sanctify them in the truth; your word is truth. ¹⁸ As you have sent me into the world, so I have sent them into the world.

***Get yourselves
a new heart . . .***

O Almighty God,
we humbly ask you
to make us like trees
planted by the waterside,
that we may bear fruits
of good living in due season.
Forgive our past offenses,
sanctify us now,
and direct all that we should be
in the future,
for Christ's sake. Amen.

–Prayer from Nigeria

---

*Wash me thoroughly from my iniquity,
and cleanse me from my sin.*
— Psalm 51:2

8

SATURDAY AFTER ASH WEDNESDAY

_____

_____

_____

_____

First Reading: Ezekiel 39:21–29

_____

25 Therefore thus says the Lord GOD:
Now I will restore the fortunes of Jacob,
and have mercy on the whole house of
Israel; and I will be jealous for my holy
name. 26 They shall forget their shame,
and all the treachery they have practiced
against me, when they live securely in
their land with no one to make them
afraid, 27 when I have brought them back
from the peoples and gathered them from
their enemies' lands, and through them
have displayed my holiness in the sight of
many nations.

_____

_____

Second Reading: Philippines 4:10–20

19 And my God will fully satisfy every
need of yours according to his riches in
glory in Christ Jesus.

Gospel: John 17:20–26

22 The glory that you have
given me I have given them,
so that they may be one, as we
are one, 23 I in them and you
in me, that they may become
completely one, so that the
world may know that you have
sent me and have loved them
even as you have loved me.

You desire truth in the inward being;
therefore teach me wisdom in my secret heart.
—Psalm 51:6

FIRST SUNDAY
IN LENT

First Reading:
Genesis 2:7–9, 15–17; 3:1–7

⁶ So when the woman saw that the tree was good for food, and that it was a delight to the eyes, and that the tree was to be desired to make one wise, she took of its fruit and ate; and she also gave some to her husband, who was with her, and he ate. ⁷ Then the eyes of both were opened, and they knew that they were naked; and they sewed fig leaves together and made loincloths for themselves.

Second Reading:
Romans 5:12 (13–16) 17–19

¹⁵ But the free gift is not like the trespass. For if the many died through the one man's trespass, much more surely have the grace of God and the free gift in the grace of the one man, Jesus Christ, abounded for the many. ¹⁶ And the free gift is not like the effect of the one man's sin. For the judgment following one trespass brought condemnation, but the free gift following many trespasses brings justification. ¹⁷ If, because of the one man's trespass, death exercised dominion through that one, much more surely will those who received the abundance of grace and the free gift of righteousness exercise dominion in life through the one man, Jesus Christ.

Our greatest glory is not in never falling but in rising every time we fall.
                                                            —Confucius

---

**Gospel:
Matthew 4:1–11**

[1] Then Jesus was led up by the Spirit into the wilderness to be tempted by the devil. [2] He fasted forty days and forty nights, and afterwards he was famished. [3] The tempter came and said to him, "If you are the Son of God, command these stones to become loaves of bread." [4] But he answered, "It is written,

'One does not live by bread alone,
    but by every word that comes
        from the mouth of God.'"

Jesus, be the canoe . . .

O Jesus,
be the canoe
    that holds me up in the sea of life;
be the rudder
    that keeps me in the straight road;
be the outrigger
    that supports me in times of temptation.
Let your Spirit be my sail
    that carries me through each day.
Keep my body strong,
so I can paddle steadfastly on
in the voyage of life.
Amen.
                    –A Melanesian islander's prayer

11

Gospel: Mark 1:1–13

[4] John the baptizer appeared in the wilderness, proclaiming a baptism of repentance for the forgiveness of sins. [5] And people from the whole Judean countryside and all the people of Jerusalem were going out to him, and were baptized by him in the river Jordan, confessing their sins. [6] Now John was clothed with camel's hair, with a leather belt around his waist, and he ate locusts and wild honey. [7] He proclaimed, "The one who is more powerful than I is coming after me; I am not worthy to stoop down and untie the thong of his sandals. [8] I have baptized you with water; but he will baptize you with the Holy Spirit."

[9] In those days Jesus came from Nazareth of Galilee and was baptized by John in the Jordan. [10] And just as he was coming up out of the water, he saw the heavens torn apart and the Spirit descending like a dove on him. [11] Then a voice came from heaven, "You are my Son, the Beloved; with you I am well pleased."

First Reading: Genesis 37:1–11

[5] Once Joseph had a dream, and when he told it to his brothers, they hated him even more.

Second Reading: 1 Corinthians 1:1–19

[18] For the message about the cross is foolishness to those who are perishing, but to us who are being saved it is the power of God.

Out of the depths I cry to you, O Lord.
Lord, hear my voice!
—Psalm 130:1–2

TUESDAY OF THE
FIRST WEEK IN LENT

_____

_____

_____

_____

First Reading: Genesis 37:12–24

_____

[19] They said to one another, "Here comes this dreamer. [20] Come now, let us kill him and throw him into one of the pits...."

Gospel: Mark 1:14–28

Second Reading: 1 Corinthians 1:20–31

[26] Consider your own call, brothers and sisters: not many of you were wise by human standards, not many were powerful, not many were of noble birth. [27] But God chose what is foolish in the world to shame the wise; God chose what is weak in the world to shame the strong; [28] God chose what is low and despised in the world, things that are not, to reduce to nothing things that are, [29] so that no one might boast in the presence of God. [30] He is the source of your life in Christ Jesus, who became for us wisdom from God, and righteousness and sanctification and redemption, [31] in order that, as it is written, "Let the one who boasts, boast in the Lord."

[14] Now after John was arrested, Jesus came to Galilee, proclaiming the good news of God, [15] and saying, "The time is fulfilled, and the kingdom of God has come near; repent, and believe in the good news." [16] As Jesus passed along the Sea of Galilee, he saw Simon and his brother Andrew casting a net into the sea — for they were fishermen. [17] And Jesus said to them, "Follow me and I will make you fish for people." [18] And immediately they left their nets and followed him. [19] As he went a little farther, he saw James son of Zebedee and his brother John, who were in their boat mending the nets. [20] Immediately he called them; and they left their father Zebedee in the boat with the hired men, and followed him. [21] They went to Capernaum; and when the sabbath came, he entered the synagogue and taught. [22] They were astounded at his teaching, for he taught them as one having authority, and not as the scribes.

_____

_____

_____

_____

Let your ears be attentive
to the voice of my supplications!
— Psalm 130:2

13

_____
_____
_____
_____
_____
_____
_____
_____

Gospel: Mark 1:29–45

²⁹ As soon as they left the synagogue, they entered the house of Simon and Andrew, with James and John. ³⁰ Now Simon's mother-in-law was in bed with a fever, and they told him about her at once. ³¹ He came and took her by the hand and lifted her up. Then the fever left her, and she began to serve them.

³² That evening, at sundown, they brought to him all who were sick or possessed with demons. ³³ And the whole city was gathered around the door. ³⁴ And he healed many who were sick with various diseases, and cast out many demons; and he would not permit the demons to speak, because they knew him.

³⁵ In the morning, while it was still very dark, he got up and went out to a deserted place, and there he prayed. ³⁶ And Simon and his companions hunted for him. ³⁷ When they found him, they said to him, "Everyone is searching for you." ³⁸ He answered, "Let us go on to the neighboring towns, so that I may proclaim the message there also; for that is what I came out to do." ³⁹ And he went throughout Galilee, proclaiming the message in their synagogues and casting out demons.

First Reading:
Genesis 37:25–36

²⁸ When some Midianite traders passed by, they drew Joseph up, lifting him out of the pit, and sold him to the Ishmaelites for twenty pieces of silver. And they took Joseph to Egypt.

Second Reading:
1 Corinthians 2:1–13

² For I decided to know nothing among you except Jesus Christ, and him crucified.

If you, O LORD, should mark iniquities,
  Lord, who could stand?
But there is forgiveness with you,
  so that you may be revered.
          — Psalm 130:3–4

14

THURSDAY OF THE FIRST WEEK IN LENT

_____

_____

_____

_____

_____

Gospel: Mark 2:1–12

_____

¹ When he returned to Capernaum after some days, it was reported that he was at home. ² So many gathered around that there was no longer room for them, not even in front of the door; and he was speaking the word to them. ³ Then some people came, bringing to him a paralyzed man, carried by four of them. ⁴ And when they could not bring him to Jesus because of the crowd, they removed the roof above him; and after having dug through it, they let down the mat on which the paralytic lay. ⁵ When Jesus saw their faith, he said to the paralytic, "Son, your sins are forgiven." ⁶ Now some of the scribes were sitting there, questioning in their hearts, ⁷ "Why does this fellow speak in this way? It is blasphemy! Who can forgive sins but God alone?" ⁸ At once Jesus perceived in his spirit that they were discussing these questions among themselves; and he said to them, "Why to you raise such questions in your hearts? ⁹ Which is easier, to say to the paralytic, 'Your sins are forgiven,' or to say, 'Stand up and take your mat and walk'? ¹⁰ But so that you may know that the Son of Man has authority on earth to forgive sins" — he said to the paralytic — ¹¹ "I say to you, stand up, take your mat and go to your home." ¹² And he stood up, and immediately took the mat and went out before all of them; so that they were all amazed and glorified God, saying, "We have never seen anything like this!"

_____

_____

_____

_____

_____

_____

_____

_____

_____

_____

First Reading: Genesis 39:1–23

² The LORD was with Joseph, and he became a successful man; he was in the house of his Egyptian master.

Second Reading: 1 Corinthians 2:14–3:15

⁹ For we are God's servants, working together; you are God's field, God's building.

I wait for the LORD,
my soul waits....
— Psalm 130:5

15

FRIDAY OF THE FIRST WEEK IN LENT

Second Reading: 1 Corinthians 3:16–23

[18] Do not deceive yourselves. If you think that you are wise in this age, you should become fools so that you may become wise. [19] For the wisdom of this world is foolishness with God.... [21] So let no one boast about human leaders. For all things are yours, [22] whether Paul or Apollos or Cephas or the world or life or death or the present or the future — all belong to you, [23] and you belong to Christ, and Christ belongs to God.

Gospel: Mark 2:13–22

[15] And as he sat at dinner in Levi's house, many tax collectors and sinners were also sitting with Jesus and his disciples — for there were many who followed him. [16] When the scribes of the Pharisees saw that he was eating with sinners and tax collectors, they said to his disciples, "Why does he eat with tax collectors and sinners?" [17] When Jesus heard this, he said to them, "Those who are well have no need of a physician, but those who are sick; I have come to call not the righteous but sinners."

First Reading: Genesis 40:1–23

[8] They said to him, "We have had dreams, and there is no one to interpret them." And Joseph said to them, "Do not interpretations belong to God? Please tell them to me."

...my soul waits for the Lord more than those who watch for the morning....
—Psalm 130:6

SATURDAY OF THE FIRST WEEK IN LENT

_____
_____
_____

First Reading: Genesis 41:1–13

¹²A young Hebrew was there with us, a servant of the captain of the guard. When we told him, he interpreted our dreams to us, giving an interpretation to each according to his dream.

Second Reading: 1 Corinthians 4:1–7

¹Think of us in this way, as servants of Christ and stewards of God's mysteries.

Gospel: Mark 2:23–3:6

²³One sabbath he was going through the grainfields; and as they made their way his disciples began to pluck heads of grain. ²⁴The Pharisees said to him, "Look, why are they doing what is not lawful on the sabbath?" ²⁵And he said to them, "Have you never read what David did when he and his companions were hungry and in need of food? ²⁶He entered the house of God, when Abiathar was high priest, and ate the bread of the Presence, which it is not lawful for any but the priests to eat, and he gave some to his companions." ²⁷Then he said to them, "The sabbath was made for humankind, and not humankind for the sabbath; ²⁸so the Son of Man is lord even of the sabbath."

O Israel, hope in the LORD!
For with the LORD there is steadfast love....
—Psalm 130:7–8

SECOND SUNDAY
IN LENT

this
is what
Yahweh
asks of you,
to act
Justly,
to love
tenderly,
and to walk
humbly
with your
God.

micah:6

First Reading: Genesis 12:1–8

[1] Now the LORD said to Abram, "Go from your country and your kindred and your father's house to the land that I will show you. [2] I will make of you a great nation, and I will bless you, and make your name great, so that you will be a blessing. [3] I will bless those who bless you, and the one who curses you I will curse; and in you all the families of the earth shall be blessed."

Second Reading: Romans 4:1–5, 13–17

[13] For the promise that he would inherit the world did not come to Abraham or to his descendants through the law but through the righteousness of faith. [14] If it is the adherents of the law who are to be the heirs, faith is null and the promise is void. [15] For the law brings wrath; but where there is no law, neither is there violation.

[16] For this reason, it depends on faith, in order that the promise may rest on grace and be guaranteed to all his descendants, not only to the adherents of the law but also to those who share the faith of Abraham (for he is the father of all of us, [17] as it is written, "I have made you the father of many nations") — in the presence of the God in whom he believed, who gives life to the dead and calls into existence the things that do not exist.

God wants to be known and loved through justice and compassion.

— Julian of Norwich

Gospel: John 4:5–26 (27–30, 39–42)

[27] Just then his disciples came. They were astonished that he was speaking with a woman, but no one said, "What do you want?" or, "Why are you speaking with her?" [28] Then the woman left her water jar and went back to the city. She said to the people, [29] "Come and see a man who told me everything I have ever done! He cannot be the Messiah, can he?" [30] They left the city and were on their way to him. . . .

[39] Many Samaritans from that city believed in him because of the woman's testimony, "He told me everything I have ever done."

I believe, but increase my faith

I believe, although everything hides you from my faith.
I believe, although everything shouts No! to me,
because I have based my faith on an unchangeable God,
a God who does not change, a God who is love. . . .

I believe, although everything revolts my being.
I believe, although I feel alone in pain,
because a Christian who has the Lord for Friend
does not waver in doubt, stands fast in faith.

I believe, although I see men hating.
I believe, although I see children weep,
because I have learnt with certainty that he comes to meet us
in the hardest hours, with his love and his light.

I believe, but increase my faith.

–Livro de Cantos, Centro Social Pe. João Cálabria,
Porte Alegre, Brazil

19

MONDAY OF THE SECOND WEEK IN LENT

_____

_____

**First Reading:
Genesis 41:46–57**

55 When all the land of Egypt was famished, the people cried to Pharaoh for bread. Pharaoh said to all the Egyptians, "Go to Joseph; what he says to you, do."

**Second Reading:
1 Corinthians 4:8–20 (21)**

10 We are fools for the sake of Christ, but you are wise in Christ. We are weak, but you are strong. You are held in honor, but we in disrepute. 11 To the present hour we are hungry and thirsty, we are poorly clothed and beaten and homeless, 12 and we grow weary from the work of our own hands. When reviled, we bless; when persecuted, we endure; 13 when slandered, we speak kindly. We have become like the rubbish of the world, the dregs of all things, to this very day.

O give thanks to the LORD. . . .
— Psalm 105:1

Gospel: Mark 3:7–19a

7 Jesus departed with his disciples to the sea, and a great multitude from Galilee followed him; 8 hearing all that he was doing, they came to him in great numbers from Judea, Jerusalem, Idumea, beyond the Jordan, and the region around Tyre and Sidon. 9 He told his disciples to have a boat ready for him because of the crowd, so that they would not crush him; 10 for he had cured many, so that all who had diseases pressed upon him to touch him. 11 Whenever the unclean spirits saw him, they fell down before him and shouted, "You are the Son of God!" 12 But he sternly ordered them not to make him known.

13 He went up the mountain and called to him those whom he wanted, and they came to him. 14 And he appointed twelve, whom he also named apostles, to be with him, and to be sent out to proclaim the message, 15 and to have authority to cast out demons. 16 So he appointed the twelve: Simon (to whom he gave the name Peter); 17 James son of Zebedee and John the brother of James (to whom he gave the name Boanerges, that is, Sons of Thunder); 18 and Andrew, and Philip, and Bartholomew, and Matthew, and Thomas, and James son of Alphaeus, and Thaddaeus, and Simon the Cananaean, 19 and Judas Iscariot, who betrayed him.

TUESDAY OF THE SECOND WEEK IN LENT

First Reading: Genesis 42:1–17

⁶ Now Joseph was governor over the land; it was he who sold to all the people of the land. And Joseph's brothers came and bowed themselves before him with their faces to the ground.

Second Reading: 1 Corinthians 5:1–8

⁶ Do you not know that a little yeast leavens the whole batch of dough? ⁷ Clean out the old yeast so that you may be a new batch, as you really are unleavened. For our paschal lamb, Christ, has been sacrificed. ⁸ Therefore, let us celebrate the festival, not with the old yeast, the yeast of malice and evil, but with the unleavened bread of sincerity and truth.

Gospel: Mark 3:19b–35

³¹ Then his mother and his brothers came; and standing outside, they sent to him and called him. ³² A crowd was sitting around him, and they said to him; "Your mother and your brothers and sisters are outside, asking for you." ³³ And he replied, "Who are my mother and my brothers?" ³⁴ And looking at those who sat around him, he said, "Here are my mother and my brothers! ³⁵ Whoever does the will of God is my brother and sister and mother."

"I will follow you"

I will follow you, Jesus,
And I will give you all
For by your strength
I will follow you in everything.
–Congolese hymn

...let the hearts of those who seek the LORD rejoice.
— Psalm 105:3

21

Gospel: Mark 4:1–20

[3] Listen! A sower went out to sow. [4] And as he sowed, some seed fell on the path, and the birds came and ate it up. [5] Other seed fell on rocky ground, where it did not have much soil, and it sprang up quickly, since it had no depth of soil. [6] And when the sun rose, it was scorched; and since it had no root, it withered away. [7] Other seed fell among thorns, and the thorns grew up and choked it, and it yielded no grain. [8] Other seed fell into good soil and brought forth grain, growing up and increasing and yielding thirty and sixty and a hundredfold.... [14] The sower sows the word. [15] These are the ones on the path where the word is sown: when they hear, Satan immediately comes and takes away the word that is sown in them. [16] And these are the ones sown on rocky ground: when they hear the word, they immediately receive it with joy. [17] But they have no root, and endure only for a while; then, when trouble or persecution arises on account of the word, immediately they fall away. [18] And others are those sown among the thorns: these are the ones who hear the word, [19] but the cares of the world, and the lure of wealth, and the desire for other things, come in and choke the word, and it yields nothing. [20] And these are the ones sown on the good soil: they hear the word and accept it and bear fruit, thirty and sixty and a hundredfold.

**First Reading:
Genesis 42:18–28**

[18] On the third day Joseph said to them, "Do this and you will live, for I fear God: [19] if you are honest men, let one of your brothers stay here where you are imprisoned. The rest of you shall go and carry grain for the famine of your households, [20] and bring your youngest brother to me. Thus your words will be verified, and you shall not die." And they agreed to do so.

**Second Reading:
1 Corinthians 5:9–6:11**

[11] And this is what some of you used to be. But you were washed, you were sanctified, you were justified in the name of the Lord Jesus Christ and in the Spirit of our God.

Seek the LORD....
— Psalm 105:4

THURSDAY OF THE SECOND WEEK IN LENT

_____

_____

_____

_____

_____

_____

_____

_____

_____

_____

_____

_____

_____

_____

Gospel: Mark 4:21–34

²¹ He said to them, "Is a lamp brought in to be put under the bushel basket, or under the bed, and not on the lampstand? ²² For there is nothing hidden, except to be disclosed; nor is anything secret, except to come to light. ²³ Let anyone with ears to hear listen!" . . . ²⁶ He also said, "The kingdom of God is as if someone would scatter seed on the ground, ²⁷ and would sleep and rise night and day, and the seed would sprout and grow, he does not know how. ²⁸ The earth produces of itself, first the stalk, then the head, then the full grain in the head. ²⁹ But when the grain is ripe, at once he goes in with his sickle, because the harvest has come."

³⁰ He also said, 'With what can we compare the kingdom of God, or what parable will we use for it? ³¹ It is like a mustard seed, which, when sown upon the ground, is the smallest of all the seeds on earth; ³² yet when it is sown it grows up and becomes the greatest of all shrubs, and puts forth large branches, so that the birds of the air can make nests in its shade."

First Reading: Genesis 42:29–38

²⁹ When they came to their father Jacob in the land of Canaan, they told him all that had happened to them. . . .

Second Reading: 1 Corinthians 6:12–20

¹⁹ Or do you not know that your body is a temple of the Holy Spirit within you, which you have from God, and that you are not your own? ²⁰ For you were bought with a price; therefore glorify God in your body.

FRIDAY OF THE SECOND WEEK IN LENT

_____

First Reading: Genesis 43:1–15

_____

¹⁵ . . . Then they went on their way down to Egypt, and stood before Joseph.

_____

Second Reading: 1 Corinthians 7:1–9

_____

⁷ . . . each has a particular gift from God, one having one kind and another a different kind.

_____

Gospel: Mark 4:35–41

_____

³⁷ A great windstorm arose, and the waves beat into the boat, so that the boat was already being swamped. ³⁸ But he was in the stern, asleep on the cushion; and they woke him up and said to him, "Teacher, do you not care that we are perishing?" ³⁹ He woke up and rebuked the wind, and said to the sea, "Peace! Be still!" Then the wind ceased, and there was a dead calm. ⁴⁰ He said to them, "Why are you afraid? Have you still no faith?" ⁴¹ And they were filled with great awe and said to one another, "Who then is this, that even the wind and the sea obey him?"

We are lost!
Do you not care?

Lord Jesus, you were awakened by the cry of your disciples on a storm-tossed sea. Hear also our cry for help. There is no justice in our land for the weak and the powerless, because the powerful and the strong have decided what is and what is not right and just. We, the minority of the humble and weak, are tired of crying for justice and peace. How much longer must the strong dominate and the weak suffer? Bring your justice and grant us your peace. Let your kingdom become a reality on this earth.

–A prayer from Sri Lanka

I will sing to the LORD as long as I live. . . .
— Psalm 104:33

SATURDAY OF THE SECOND WEEK IN LENT

_____
_____
_____
_____

Gospel: Mark 5:1–20

²And when he had stepped out of the boat, immediately a man out of the tombs with an unclean spirit met him. ³He lived among the tombs; and no one could restrain him any more, even with a chain; ⁴for he had often been restrained with shackles and chains, but the chains he wrenched apart, and the shackles he broke in pieces; and no one had the strength to subdue him. ⁵Night and day among the tombs and on the mountains he was always howling and bruising himself with stones. ⁶When he saw Jesus from a distance, he ran and bowed down before him; ⁷and he shouted at the top of his voice, "What have you to do with me, Jesus, Son of the Most High God? I adjure you by God, do not torment me." ⁸For he had said to him, "Come out of the man, you unclean spirit!" ⁹Then Jesus asked him, "What is your name?" He replied, "My name is Legion; for we are many." ¹⁰He begged him earnestly not to send them out of the country. ¹¹Now there on the hillside a great herd of swine was feeding; ¹²and the unclean spirits begged him, "Send us into the swine; let us enter them." ¹³So he gave them permission. And the unclean spirits came out and entered the swine; and the herd, numbering about two thousand, rushed down the steep bank into the sea, and were drowned in the sea.

Happy are those who observe justice....
— Psalm 106:3

First Reading: Genesis 43:16–34

¹⁶When Joseph saw Benjamin with them, he said to the steward of his house, "Bring the men into the house, and slaughter an animal and make ready, for the men are to dine with me at noon."

Second Reading: 1 Corinthians 7:10–24

²³You were bought with a price; do not become slaves of human masters.

My name is Legion; for we are many.

The announcement of the gospel implies the _denunciation_ of everything that is not in agreement with the gospel. No evangelism is authentically evangelical if it is not at the same time prophetic. The church cannot make a compromise with any force that oppresses or dehumanizes human beings. It cannot name Jesus Christ if it does not name also the idols and the demons that must be cast out from the inner life of humankind and from the structures of society.
— _"Manifesto to the Nation," Evangelical Methodist Church in Bolivia_

THIRD SUNDAY
IN LENT

_____

_____

First Reading: Isaiah 42:14–21

_____

[16] I will lead the blind
  by a road they do not know,
by paths they have not known
  I will guide them.
I will turn the darkness before them into
    light,
  the rough places into level ground.
These are the things I will do,
  and I will not forsake them....
Listen, you that are deaf;
  and you that are blind, look up and see!

healing-people
whose hands
  touch others
into life and
well-being,
struggling
always against the
forces of death

For all peoples, that thy light may shine upon them,
that the spirit of justice and mutual forbearance
may be established among them,
the spirit of love and peace.
—Melkite petition

Second Reading: Ephesians 5:8–14

[8] For once you were darkness, but now in the Lord you are light. Live as children of light — [9] for the fruit of the light is found in all that is good and right and true. [10] Try to find out what is pleasing to the Lord. [11] Take no part in the unfruitful works of darkness, but instead expose them. [12] For it is shameful even to mention what such people do secretly; [13] but everything exposed by the light becomes visible, [14] for everything that becomes visible is light. Therefore it says,
   "Sleeper, awake!
      Rise from the dead,
   and Christ will shine on you."

Look up and see . . .
O Creator and Mighty God,
   you have promised
   strength for the weak
   rest for the laborers
   light for the way
   grace for the trials
   help from above
   unfailing sympathy
   undying love.
O Creator and Mighty God
help us to continue in your promise.
   Amen.
   –Prayer from Pakistan

Gospel: John 9:1–41

[13] They brought to the Pharisees the man who had formerly been blind. [14] Now it was a sabbath day when Jesus made the mud and opened his eyes. [15] Then the Pharisees also began to ask him how he had received his sight. He said to them, "He put mud on my eyes. Then I washed, and now I see." [16] Some of the Pharisees said, "This man is not from God, for he does not observe the sabbath." But others said, "How can a man who is a sinner perform such signs?" [17] So they said again to the blind man, "What do you say about him? It was your eyes he opened." He said, "He is a prophet." . . .

[39] Jesus said, "I came into this world for judgment so that those who do not see may see, and those who do see may become blind." [40] Some of the Pharisees near him heard this and said to him, "Surely we are not blind, are we?"

MONDAY OF THE THIRD WEEK IN LENT

Gospel: Mark 5:21–43

[24] And a large crowd followed him and pressed in on him. [25] Now there was a woman who had been suffering from hemorrhages for twelve years. [26] She had endured much under many physicians, and had spent all that she had; and she was no better, but rather grew worse. [27] She had heard about Jesus, and came up behind him in the crowd and touched his cloak, [28] for she said, "If I but touch his clothes, I will be made well." [29] Immediately her hemorrhage stopped; and she felt in her body that she was healed of her disease. [30] Immediately aware that power had gone forth from him, Jesus turned about in the crowd and said, "Who touched my clothes?" [31] And his disciples said to him, "You see the crowd pressing in on you; how can you say, 'Who touched me?'" [32] He looked all around to see who had done it. [33] But the woman, knowing what had happened to her, came in fear and trembling, fell down before him, and told him the whole truth. [34] He said to her, "Daughter, your faith has made you well; go in peace, and be healed of your disease."

First Reading:
Genesis 44:18–34

[34] "... For how can I go back to my father if the boy is not with me? I fear to see the suffering that would come upon my father."

Second Reading:
1 Corinthians 7:25–31

[31] ... For the present form of this world is passing away.

Even the merest gesture is holy if it is filled with faith.   *–Franz Kafka*

With my voice I cry to the LORD;
with my voice I make supplication to the LORD.
                              —Psalm 142:1

28

TUESDAY OF THE THIRD WEEK IN LENT

Gospel: Mark 6:1–13

[2] On the sabbath he began to teach in the synagogue, and many who heard him were astounded. They said, "Where did this man get all this? What is this wisdom that has been given to him? What deeds of power have been done by his hands! [3] Is not this the carpenter, the son of Mary and brother of James and Joses and Judas and Simon, and are not his sisters here with us?" And they took offense at him. [4] Then Jesus said to them, "Prophets are not without honor, except in their hometown, and among their own kin, and in their own house." . . . [7] He called the twelve and began to send them out two by two, and gave them authority over the unclean spirits. [8] He ordered them to take nothing for their journey except a staff; no bread, no bag, no money in their belts; [9] but to wear sandals and not to put on two tunics. [10] He said to them, "Wherever you enter a house, stay there until you leave the place. [11] If any place will not welcome you and they refuse to hear you, when you leave, shake off the dust that is on your feet as a testimony against them." [12] So they went out and proclaimed that all should repent. [13] They cast out many demons, and anointed with oil many who were sick and cured them.

**First Reading:
Genesis 45:1–15**

[4] Then Joseph said to his brothers, "Come closer to me." And they came closer. He said, "I am your brother, Joseph, whom you sold into Egypt. . . . "

**Second Reading:
1 Corinthians 7:32–40**

[32] I want you to be free from anxieties. . . .

He ordered them to take nothing for their journey except a staff . . .

O God, we do not protest even if our life is destined to lead to the cross, or if the way leads to our losing our lives. Teach us how to dispense with unnecessary things.

–Toyohiko Kagawa

_____
_____
_____
_____
_____
_____
_____
_____
_____
_____
_____
_____

**First Reading:
Genesis 45:16–28**

_____

[28] Israel said, "Enough! My son Joseph is still alive. I must go and see him before I die."

_____

**Second Reading:
1 Corinthians 8:1–13**

_____

[1] . . . Knowledge puffs up, but love builds up.

*When my spirit is faint,
you know my way.*
— Psalm 142:3

Gospel: Mark 6:13–29

[21] But an opportunity came when Herod on his birthday gave a banquet for his courtiers and officers and for the leaders of Galilee. [22] When his daughter Herodias came in and danced, she pleased Herod and his guests; and the king said to the girl, "Ask me for whatever you wish, and I will give it." [23] And he solemnly swore to her, "Whatever you ask me, I will give you, even half of my kingdom." [24] She went out and said to her mother, "What should I ask for?" She replied, "The head of John the baptizer." [25] Immediately she rushed back to the king and requested, "I want you to give me at once the head of John the Baptist on a platter." [26] The king was deeply grieved; yet out of regard for his oaths and for the guests, he did not want to refuse her. [27] Immediately the king sent a soldier of the guard with orders to bring John's head. He went and beheaded him in the prison, [28] brought his head on a platter, and gave it to the girl. Then the girl gave it to her mother.

THURSDAY OF THE THIRD WEEK IN LENT

_____

_____

_____

_____

_____

_____

Gospel: Mark 6:30–46

³⁴ As he went ashore, he saw a great crowd; and he had compassion for them, because they were like sheep without a shepherd; and he began to teach them many things. ³⁵ When it grew late, his disciples came to him and said, "This is a deserted place, and the hour is now very late; ³⁶ send them away so that they may go into the surrounding country and villages and buy something for themselves to eat." ³⁷ But he answered them, "You give them something to eat." They said to him, "Are we to go and buy two hundred denarii worth of bread, and give it to them to eat?" ³⁸ And he said to them, "How many loaves have you? Go and see." When they had found out, they said, "Five, and two fish." ³⁹ Then he ordered them to get all the people to sit down in groups on the green grass. ⁴⁰ So they sat down in groups of hundreds and of fifties. ⁴¹ Taking the five loaves and the two fish, he looked up to heaven, and blessed and broke the loaves, and gave them to his disciples to set before the people; and he divided the two fish among them all. ⁴² And all ate and were filled; ⁴³ and they took up twelve baskets full of broken pieces and of the fish.

_____

First Reading:
Genesis 46:1–7, 28–34

³⁰ Israel said to Joseph, "I can die now, having seen for myself that you are still alive."

_____

Second Reading:
1 Corinthians 9:1–15

⁴ Do we not have the right to our food and drink?

Sharing the same bread

You have come from afar
and waited long
and are wearied:
Let us sit side by side
sharing the same bread
drawn from the same source
to quiet the same hunger
that makes us weak.
Then standing together
let us share the same spirit,
the same thoughts
that once again draw us
together in friendship
and unity and peace.
    –Prières d'Ozawamick,
    Canadian Indian liturgical text

I cry to you, O LORD;
   I say, "You are my refuge,
   my portion in the land of the living."
      — Psalm 142:5

FRIDAY OF THE THIRD WEEK IN LENT

**First Reading:
Genesis 47:1–26**

[11] Joseph settled his father and his brothers, and granted them a holding in the land of Egypt, in the best part of the land, in the land of Rameses, as Pharaoh had instructed. [12] And Joseph provided his father, his brothers, and all his father's household with food, according to the number of their dependents.

**Second Reading:
1 Corinthians 9:16–27**

[24] Do you not know that in a race the runners all compete, but only one receives the prize? Run in such a way that you may win it. [25] Athletes exercise self-control in all things; they do it to receive a perishable wreath, but we an imperishable one. [26] So I do not run aimlessly, nor do I box as though beating the air; [27] but I punish my body and enslave it, so that after proclaiming to others I myself should not be disqualified.

*Give heed to my cry,
    for I am brought very low.*
        —Psalm 142:6

Gospel: Mark 6:47–56

[47] When evening came, the boat was out on the sea, and he was alone on the land. [48] When he saw that they were straining at the oars against an adverse wind, he came towards them early in the morning, walking on the sea. He intended to pass them by. [49] But when they saw him walking on the sea, they thought it was a ghost and cried out; [50] for they all saw him and were terrified. But immediately he spoke to them and said, "Take heart, it is I; do not be afraid." [51] Then he got into the boat with them and the wind ceased. And they were utterly astounded, [52] for they did not understand about the loaves, but their hearts were hardened.

[53] When they had crossed over, they came to land at Gennesaret and moored the boat. [54] When they got out of the boat, people at once recognized him, [55] and rushed about that whole region and began to bring the sick on mats to wherever they heard he was. [56] And wherever he went, into villages or cities or farms, they laid the sick in the marketplaces, and begged him that they might touch even the fringe of his cloak; and all who touched it were healed.

SATURDAY OF THE THIRD WEEK IN LENT

**First Reading:
Genesis 47:27–48:7**

³ And Jacob said to Joseph, "God Almighty appeared to me at Luz in the land of Canaan, and he blessed me, ⁴ and said to me, 'I am going to make you fruitful and increase your numbers; I will make of you a company of peoples, and will give this land to your offspring after you for a perpetual holding.'"

Second Reading: 1 Corinthians 10:1–13

¹² So if you think you are standing, watch out that you do not fall. ¹³ No testing has overtaken you that is not common to everyone. God is faithful, and he will not let you be tested beyond your strength, but with the testing he will also provide the way out so that you may be able to endure it.

Gospel: Mark 7:1–23

¹⁸ ... "Then do you also fail to understand? Do you not see that whatever goes into a person from outside cannot defile, ¹⁹ since it enters, not the heart but the stomach, and goes out into the sewer?" (Thus he declared all foods clean.) ²⁰ And he said, "It is what comes out of a person that defiles. ²¹ For it is from within, from the human heart, that evil intentions come: fornication, theft, murder, ²² adultery, avarice, wickedness, deceit, licentiousness, envy, slander, pride, folly. ²³ All these evil things come from within, and they defile a person."

> **. . . it is from within . . .**
> Truth lies waiting in all things —
> unfolding itself from living buds.
> But first it must be in yourself.
> It shall come from your soul. It
> shall be love.
> —*Walt Whitman*

*Bring me out of prison,
so that I may give thanks
to your name.*
— Psalm 142:7

FOURTH SUNDAY IN LENT

First Reading: Hosea 5:15–6:2

[1] "Come, let us return to the
LORD;
for it is he who has torn,
and he will heal us;
he has struck down, and he
will bind us up.
[2] After two days he will revive
us;
on the third day he will
raise us up,
that we may live before
him...."

Second Reading: Romans 8:1–10

[5] For those who live according to the flesh
set their minds on the things of the flesh,
but those who live according to the Spirit
set their minds on the things of the Spirit.
[6] To set the mind on the flesh is death,
but to set the mind on the Spirit is life
and peace. [7] For this reason the
mind that is set on the flesh
is hostile to God; it does
not submit to God's
law — indeed
it cannot, [8] and
those who are in
the flesh cannot
please God.
[9] But you are
not in the flesh;
you are in the
Spirit, since
the Spirit of
God dwells in
you. Anyone
who does not
have the Spirit
of Christ does
not belong to
him. [10] But if
Christ is in you,
though the body
is dead because
of sin, the Spirit
is life because of
righteousness.

...there will always be those who cannot live with themselves at the expense of fullness of life for others.
— Nadine Gordimer

Gospel: Matthew 20:17–28

[17] While Jesus was going up to Jerusalem, he took the twelve disciples aside by themselves, and said to them on the way, [18] "See, now we are going up to Jerusalem; and the Son of Man will be handed over to the chief priests and scribes, and they will condemn him to death; [19] then they will hand him over to the Gentiles to be mocked and flogged and crucified; and on the third day he will be raised up." [20] Then the mother of the sons of Zebedee came to him with her sons, and kneeling before him, she asked a favor of him. [21] And he said to her, "What do you want?" She said to him, "Declare that these two sons of mine will sit, one at your right hand and one at your left, in your kingdom." [22] But Jesus answered, "You do not know what you are asking. Are you able to drink the cup that I am about to drink?" They said to him, "We are able." [23] He said to them, "You will indeed drink my cup, but to sit at my right hand and at my left, this is not mine to grant, but is for those for whom it has been prepared by my Father."

I am no longer afraid of death

I am no longer afraid of death;
I know well
its dark and cold corridors
leading to life.

I am afraid rather of that life
which does not come out of
    death
which cramps our hands
and retards our march.

I am afraid of my fear
and even more of the fear
    of others,
who do not know where they
    are going,
who continue clinging
to what they consider to be life
which we know to be death!

I live each day to kill death;
I die each day to beget life,
and in this dying unto death,
I die a thousand times and
am reborn another thousand
through that love
from my People,
which nourishes hope!

–Julia Esquivel

_____

_____

Second Reading: 1 Corinthians 10:14–11:1

^{16} The cup of blessing that we bless, is it not a sharing in the blood of Christ? The bread that we break, is it not a sharing in the body of Christ? ^{17} Because there is one bread, we who are many are one body, for we all partake of the one bread.

**First Reading:
Genesis 49:1–28**

Gospel: Mark 7:24–37

^{28} All these are the twelve tribes of Israel, and this is what their father said to them when he blessed them, blessing each one of them with a suitable blessing.

^{24} From there he set out and went away to the region of Tyre. He entered a house and did not want anyone to know he was there. Yet he could not escape notice, ^{25} but a woman whose little daughter had an unclean spirit immediately heard about him, and she came and bowed down at his feet. ^{26} Now the woman was a Gentile, of Syrophoenician origin. She begged him to cast the demon out of her daughter. ^{27} He said to her, "Let the children be fed first, for it is not fair to take the children's food and throw it to the dogs." ^{28} But she answered him, "Sir, even the dogs under the table eat the children's crumbs." ^{29} Then he said to her, "For saying that, you may go — the demon has left your daughter." ^{30} So she went home, found the child lying on the bed, and the demon gone.

**We all partake
of the one bread**

Think of our world as it looks from the rocket that is heading toward Mars. It is like a child's globe, hanging in space, the continents stuck to its side like colored maps. We are all fellow passengers on a dot of earth.
–Lyndon B. Johnson

Vindicate me, O God, and defend my cause....
— Psalm 43:1

TUESDAY OF THE FOURTH WEEK IN LENT

Gospel: Mark 8:1–10

[1] In those days when there was again a great crowd without anything to eat, he called his disciples and said to them, [2] "I have compassion for the crowd, because they have been with me now for three days, and have nothing to eat. [3] If I send them away hungry to their homes, they will faint on the way — and some of them have come from a great distance." [4] His disciples replied, "How can one feed these people with bread here in the desert?" [5] He asked them, "How many loaves do you have?" They said, "Seven." [6] Then he ordered the crowd to sit down on the ground; and he took the seven loaves, and after giving thanks he broke them and gave them to this disciples to distribute; and they distributed them to the crowd. [7] They had also a few small fish; and after blessing them, he ordered that these too should be distributed. [8] They ate and were filled; and they took up the broken pieces left over, seven baskets full. [9] Now there were about four thousand people. And he sent them away. [10] And immediately he got into the boat with his disciples and went to the district of Dalmanutha.

**First Reading:
Genesis 49:29–50:14**

[14] After he had buried his father, Joseph returned to Egypt with his brothers and all who had gone up with him to bury his father.

**Second Reading:
1 Corinthians 11:2–34**

[27] Whoever, therefore, eats the bread or drinks the cup of the Lord in an unworthy manner will be answerable for the body and blood of the Lord.

**I have compassion
for the crowd**

Malnutrition is the hidden holocaust of our day. It is avoidable, and because it is avoidable it is as much an indictment of this generation of bystanders as Hitler's holocaust was an indictment of the last.

–Richard Barnet

For you are the God in whom I take refuge....
— Psalm 43:2

WEDNESDAY OF THE FOURTH WEEK IN LENT

First Reading: Genesis 50:15–26

²⁶ And Joseph died, being one hundred ten years old; he was embalmed and placed in a coffin in Egypt.

Second Reading: 1 Corinthians 12:1–11

⁴ Now there are varieties of gifts, but the same Spirit; ⁵ and there are varieties of services, but the same Lord; ⁶ and there are varieties of activities, but it is the same God who activates all of them in everyone.

Gospel: Mark 8:11–26

¹⁸ Do you have eyes, and fail to see? Do you have ears, and fail to hear? And do you not remember?

There are varieties of gifts

There is a richness in our black experience that we must share with the entire people of God. These are gifts that are part of an African past. For we have heard with black ears and we have seen with black eyes and we have understood with an African heart. We thank God . . . for the gifts of our blackness. In all humility we turn to the whole church that it might share our gifts so that "our joy may be complete."
  –*U.S. Black Catholic Bishops,
    "What We Have Seen
    and Heard"*

O send out your light and your truth;
  let them lead me. . . .
            — Psalm 43:3

THURSDAY OF THE FOURTH WEEK IN LENT

_____
_____
_____
_____
_____
_____
_____
_____

First Reading: Exodus 1:6–22

13 The Egyptians became ruthless in imposing tasks on the Israelites, 14 and made their lives bitter with hard service in mortar and brick and in every kind of field labor. They were ruthless in all the tasks that they imposed on them.

Second Reading: 1 Corinthians 12:12–26

20 As it is, there are many members, yet one body. 21 The eye cannot say to the hand, "I have no need of you," nor again the head to the feet, "I have no need of you." 22 On the contrary, the members of the body that seem to be weaker are indispensable, 23 and those members of the body that we think less honorable we clothe with greater honor, and our less respectable members are treated with greater respect; 24 whereas our more respectable members do not need this. But God has so arranged the body, giving the greater honor to the inferior member, 25 that there may be no dissension within the body, but the members may have the same care for one another. 26 If one member suffers, all suffer together with it; if one member is honored, all rejoice together with it.

Gospel: Mark 8:27–9:1

34 He called the crowd with his disciples and he said to them, "If any want to become my followers, let them deny themselves and take up their cross and follow me. 35 For those who want to save their life will lose it; and those who lose their life for my sake, and for the sake of the gospel, will save it. 36 For what will it profit them to gain the whole world and forfeit their life?

> O God
> of the ever-present crosses,
> help us, your servants.
> –Fourth-century Egyptian

_...I will go to the altar of God,
to God my exceeding joy...._
— Psalm 43:4

FRIDAY OF THE FOURTH WEEK IN LENT

_____
_____
_____
_____
_____
_____
_____
_____
_____

First Reading:
Exodus 2:1–22

^{10} When the child grew up, she brought him to Pharaoh's daughter, and she took him as her son.

Second Reading: 1 Corinthians 12:27–13:3

^{27} Now you are the body of Christ and individually members of it. ^{28} And God has appointed in the church first apostles, second prophets, third teachers; then deeds of power, then gifts of healing, forms of assistance, forms of leadership, various kinds of tongues.

Gospel: Mark 9:2–13

^{9} As they were coming down the mountain, he ordered them to tell no one about what they had seen, until after the Son of Man had risen from the dead. ^{10} So they kept the matter to themselves, questioning what this rising from the dead could mean. ^{11} Then they asked him, "Why do the scribes say that Elijah must come first?" ^{12} He said to them, "Elijah is indeed coming first to restore all things. How then is it written about the Son of Man, that he is to go through many sufferings and be treated with contempt? ^{13} But I tell you that Elijah has come, and they did to him whatever they pleased, as it is written about him."

> God creates justice in all who will be liberated through goodness.
> –_Julian of Norwich_

SATURDAY OF THE FOURTH WEEK IN LENT

_____

_____

_____

_____

_____

Second Reading: 1 Corinthians 13:1–13

^{1} If I speak in the tongues of mortals and of angels, but do not have love, I am a noisy gong or a clanging cymbal. ^{2} And if I have prophetic powers, and understand all mysteries and all knowledge, and if I have all faith, so as to remove mountains, but do not have love, I am nothing. ^{3} If I give away all my possessions, and if I hand over my body so that I may boast, but do not have love, I gain nothing. ^{4} Love is patient; love is kind; love is not envious or boastful or arrogant ^{5} or rude. It does not insist on its own way; it is not irritable or resentful; ^{6} it does not rejoice in wrongdoing, but rejoices in the truth. ^{7} It bears all things, believes all things, hopes all things, endures all things. ^{8} Love never ends. But as for prophecies, they will come to an end; as for tongues, they will cease; as for knowledge, it will come to an end. ^{9} For we know only in part, and we prophesy only in part; ^{10} but when the complete comes, the partial will come to an end. ^{11} When I was a child, I spoke like a child, I thought like a child, I reasoned like a child; when I became an adult, I put an end to childish ways. ^{12} For now we see in a mirror, dimly, but then we will see face to face. Now I know only in part; then I will know fully, even as I have been fully known. ^{13} And now faith, hope, and love abide, these three; and the greatest of these is love.

_____

_____

_____

_____

_____

_____

_____

First Reading: Exodus 2:23–3:15

^{15} God also said to Moses, "Thus you shall say to the Israelites, 'The LORD, the God of your ancestors, the God of Abraham, the God of Isaac, and the God of Jacob, has sent me to you':
This is my name forever,
this is my title for all
generations....'"

Gospel: Mark 9:14–29

^{23} Jesus said to him, "If you are able! — All things can be done for the one who believes."

_..._ _my help and my God._
—Psalm 43:5

FIFTH SUNDAY
IN LENT

First Reading: Ezekiel 37:1-3 (4-10) 11-14

[11] Then he said to me, "Mortal, these bones are the whole house of Israel. They say, 'Our bones are dried up, and our hope is lost; we are cut off completely.' [12] Therefore prophesy, and say to them, Thus says the Lord GOD: I am going to open your graves, and bring you up from your graves, O my people; and I will bring you back to the land of Israel. [13] And you shall know that I am the LORD, when I open your graves, and bring you up from your graves, O my people. . . . "

Second Reading: Romans 8:11-19

[15] For you did not receive a spirit of slavery to fall back into fear, but you have received a spirit of adoption. When we cry, "Abba! Father!" [16] it is that very Spirit bearing witness with our spirit that we are children of God, [17] and if children, then heirs, heirs of God and joint heirs with Christ — if, in fact, we suffer with him so that we may also be glorified with him. [18] I consider that the sufferings of this present time are not worth comparing with the glory about to be revealed to us. [19] For the creation waits with eager longing for the revealing of the children of God. . . .

Keep us, Sovereign Lord, from panic when crisis and panics arise. Help us to know that though you do not always remove troubles from us you always accompany us through them.

— **Prayer from Uganda**

Gospel: John 11:1–53

[38] Then Jesus, again greatly disturbed, came to the tomb. It was a cave and a stone was lying against it. [39] Jesus said, "Take away the stone." Martha, the sister of the dead man, said to him, "Lord, already there is a stench because he has been dead four days." [40] Jesus said to her, "Did I not tell you that if you believed, you would see the glory of God?" [41] So they took away the stone. And Jesus looked upward and said, "Father, I thank you for having heard me. [42] I knew that you always hear me, but I have said this for the sake of the crowd standing here, so that they may believe that you sent me." [43] ...He cried with a loud voice, "Lazarus, come out!" [44] The dead man came out, his hands and feet bound with strips of cloth, and his face wrapped in a cloth. Jesus said to them, "Unbind him, and let him go."

Lazarus, come out!

I believe you are transforming
this death-dealing world
through the Holy Spirit,
who is God's love and power.
You live raised from death,
and are present in the fight
in which we build your kingdom
of justice, peace, and love.
*–Credo from the Mass
of the Marginalized People*

_____
_____
_____
_____
_____
_____
_____
_____

Second Reading: 1 Corinthians 14:1–19

[1] Pursue love and strive for the spiritual gifts, and especially that you may prophesy. [2] For those who speak in a tongue do not speak to other people but to God; for nobody understands them, since they are speaking mysteries in the Spirit. [3] On the other hand, those who prophesy speak to other people for their upbuilding and encouragement and consolation.

**First Reading:
Exodus 4:10–20 (21–26) 27–31**

[10] But Moses said to the LORD, "O my Lord, I have never been eloquent, neither in the past nor even now that you have spoken to your servant; but I am slow of speech and slow of tongue." [11] Then the LORD said to him, "Who gives speech to mortals? Who makes them mute or deaf, seeing or blind? Is it not I, the LORD? [12] Now go, and I will be with your mouth and teach you what you are to speak."

Gospel: Mark 9:30–41

[33] Then they came to Capernaum; and when he was in the house he asked them, 'What were you arguing about on the way?" [34] But they were silent, for on the way they had argued with one another who was the greatest. [35] He sat down, called the twelve, and said to them, "Whoever wants to be first must be last of all and servant of all." [36] Then he took a little child and put it among them; and taking it in his arms, he said to them, [37] "Whoever welcomes one such child in my name welcomes me, and whoever welcomes me welcomes not me but the one who sent me."

_O LORD, I am your servant; . . .
You have loosed my bonds._
—Psalm 116:16

44

TUESDAY OF THE FIFTH WEEK IN LENT

First Reading: Exodus 5:1–6:1

[1] Afterward Moses and Aaron went to Pharaoh and said, "Thus says the LORD, the God of Israel, 'Let my people go....'"

**Second Reading:
1 Corinthians 14:20–33a, 39–40**

[20] Brothers and sisters, do not be children in your thinking; rather, be infants in evil, but in thinking be adults.

Gospel: Mark 9:42–50

[42] "If any of you put a stumbling block before one of these little ones who believe in me, it would be better for you if a great millstone were hung around your neck and you were thrown into the sea. [43] If your hand causes you to stumble, cut it off; it is better for you to enter life maimed than to have two hands and to go to hell, to the unquenchable fire. [45] And if your foot causes you to stumble, cut it off; it is better for you to enter life lame than to have two feet and to be thrown into hell...."

The snares of death encompassed me;
the pangs of Sheol laid hold on me;
I suffered distress and anguish.
Then I called on the name of the LORD:
"O LORD, I pray, save my life!"
　　　　　　　　— Psalm 116:3–4

Tomiyama Taeko

... these little ones ...
The death of one child, when the death could have been avoided, is a rebuke to all humanity.
　　　–Javier Pérez de Cuellar,
　　　U.N. Secretary General

WEDNESDAY OF THE FIFTH WEEK IN LENT

First Reading: Exodus 7:8–24

14 Then the LORD said to Moses, "Pharaoh's heart is hardened; he refuses to let the people go...."

Second Reading: 2 Corinthians 2:14–3:6

4 Such is the confidence that we have through Christ toward God. 5 Not that we are competent of ourselves to claim anything as coming from us; our competence is from God, 6 who has made us competent to be ministers of a new covenant, not of letter but of spirit; for the letter kills, but the Spirit gives life.

Let the children come to me

I saw a child today, Lord, who will not die tonight, harried into hunger's grave. He was bright and full of life because his father had a job and feeds him, but somewhere, everywhere, 10,000 life-lamps will go out, and not be lit again tomorrow. Lord, teach me my sin. Amen.
–Prayer of an African Christian

Gospel: Mark 10:1–16

13 People were bringing little children to him in order that he might touch them; and the disciples spoke sternly to them. 14 But when Jesus saw this, he was indignant and said to them, "Let the little children come to me; do not stop them; for it is to such as these that the kingdom of God belongs. 15 Truly I tell you, whoever does not receive the kingdom of God as a little child will never enter it." 16 And he took them up in his arms, laid his hands on them, and he blessed them.

The LORD protects the simple....
— Psalm 116:6

THURSDAY OF THE FIFTH WEEK IN LENT

_____
_____
_____
_____
_____

Gospel: Mark 10:17–31

[17] As he was setting out on a journey, a man ran up and knelt before him, and asked him, "Good Teacher, what must I do to inherit eternal life?" [18] Jesus said to him, "Why do you call me good? No one is good but God alone. [19] You know the commandments: 'You shall not murder. You shall not commit adultery; You shall not steal; You shall not bear false witness; You shall not defraud; Honor your father and mother.'" [20] He said to him, "Teacher, I have kept all these since my youth." [21] Jesus, looking at him, loved him and said, "You lack one thing; go, sell what you own, and give the money to the poor, and you will have treasure in heaven; then come, follow me." [22] When he heard this, he was shocked and went away grieving, for he had many possessions.

[23] Then Jesus looked around and said to his disciples, "How hard it will be for those who have wealth to enter the kingdom of God!" [24] And the disciples were perplexed at these words. But Jesus said to them again, "Children, how hard it is to enter the kingdom of God! [25] It is easier for a camel to go through the eye of a needle than for someone who is rich to enter the kingdom of God." [26] They were greatly astounded and said to one another, "Then who can be saved?" [27] Jesus looked at them and said, "For mortals it is impossible, but not for God; for God all things are possible."

What shall I return to the LORD...?
—Psalm 116:12

First Reading: Exodus 7:25–8:19

[1] Then the LORD said to Moses, "Go to Pharaoh and say to him, 'Thus says the LORD, "Let my people go, so that they may worship me. [2] If you refuse to let them go, I will plague your whole country with frogs...."

Second Reading: 2 Corinthians 3:7–18

[12] Since, then, we have such a hope, we act with great boldness.... [17] Now the Lord is the Spirit, and where the Spirit of the Lord is, there is freedom.

Sell what you own...

No wealth in the world can help humanity forward, even in the hands of the most devoted worker in this cause.... Can anyone imagine Moses, Jesus, or Gandhi armed with the money-bags of Carnegie?
–Albert Einstein

_____
_____
_____
_____
_____
_____
_____
_____
_____
_____

Second Reading: 2 Corinthians 4:1–12

⁷ But we have this treasure in clay jars, so that it may be made clear that this extraordinary power belongs to God and does not come from us. ⁸ We are afflicted in every way, but not crushed; perplexed, but not driven to despair; ⁹ persecuted, but not forsaken; struck down, but not destroyed; ¹⁰ always carrying in the body the death of Jesus, so that the life of Jesus may also be made visible in our bodies. ¹¹ For while we live, we are always being given up to death for Jesus' sake, so that the life of Jesus may be made visible in our mortal flesh. ¹² So death is at work in us, but life in you.

First Reading:
Exodus 9:13–35

¹³ Then the LORD said to Moses, "Rise early in the morning and present yourself before Pharaoh, and say to him, 'Thus says the Lord, the God of the Hebrews, Let my people go, so that they may worship me. ¹⁴ For this time I will send all my plagues upon you yourself, and upon your officials, and upon your people, so that you may know that there is no one like me in all the earth....'"

Gospel: Mark 10:32–45

³² They were on the road, going up to Jerusalem, and Jesus was walking ahead of them; they were amazed, and those who followed were afraid. He took the twelve aside again and began to tell them what was to happen to him, ³³ saying, "See, now we are going up to Jerusalem; and the Son of Man will be handed over to the chief priests and the scribes, and they will condemn him to death; then they will hand him over to the Gentiles; ³⁴ they will mock him, and spit upon him, and flog him, and kill him; and after three days he will rise again."

I will offer to you a thanksgiving sacrifice
and call on the name of the LORD.
— Psalm 116:17

48

SATURDAY OF THE FIFTH WEEK IN LENT

First Reading: Exodus 10:21–11:8

⁴ Moses said, "Thus says the LORD: About midnight I will go out through Egypt. ⁵ Every firstborn in the land of Egypt shall die, from the firstborn of Pharaoh who sits on his throne to the firstborn of the female slave who is behind the handmill, and all the firstborn of the livestock...."

Second Reading: 2 Corinthians 4:13–18

¹³ But just as we have the same spirit of faith that is in accordance with scripture — "I believed, and so I spoke" — we also believe, and so we speak, ¹⁴ because we know that the one who raised the Lord Jesus will raise us also with Jesus, and will bring us with you into his presence. ¹⁵ Yes, everything is for your sake, so that grace, as it extends to more and more people, may increase thanksgiving, to the glory of God. ¹⁶ So we do not lose heart. Even though our outer nature is wasting away, our inner nature is being renewed day by day. ¹⁷ For this slight momentary affliction is preparing us for an eternal weight of glory beyond all measure, ¹⁸ because we look not at what can be seen but at what cannot be seen; for what can be seen is temporary, but what cannot be seen is eternal.

Gospel: Mark 10:46–52

⁴⁹ Jesus stood still and said, "Call him here." And they called the blind man, saying to him, "Take heart; get up, he is calling you."

I kept my faith, even when I said,
"I am greatly afflicted."
　　　　　　—Psalm 116:10

The Cross

The cross is
  the hope of Christians
the cross is
  the resurrection of the dead
the cross is
  the way of the lost
the cross is
  the savior of the lost
the cross is
  the staff of the lame
the cross is
  the guide of the blind
the cross is
  the strength of the weak
the cross is
  the doctor of the sick
the cross is
  the aim of the priests
the cross is
  the hope of the hopeless
the cross is
  the freedom of the slaves
the cross is
  the power of the kings
the cross is
  the water of the seeds
the cross is
  the consolation of the
  bondmen
the cross is
  the source of those who
  seek water
the cross is
  the cloth of the naked.
We thank you, Father,
  for the cross.
  –Tenth-century African hymn

First Reading: Isaiah 50:4–9a

[7] The Lord GOD helps me;
  therefore I have not been disgraced;
therefore I have set my face like flint,
  and I know that I shall not be put to
    shame;
[8] he who vindicates me is near.
Who will contend with me?
  Let us stand up together.
Who are my adversaries?
  Let them confront me.
[9] It is the Lord GOD who helps me;
  who will declare me guilty?

Second Reading: Philippians 2:5–11

[5] Let the same mind be in you that was in
Christ Jesus,
  [6] who, though he was in the form of
    God,
    did not regard equality with God
    as something to be exploited,
  [7] but emptied himself,
    taking the form of a slave,
    being born in human likeness.
  And being found in human form,
[8] he humbled himself
    and became obedient to the point
      of death —
    even death on a cross.

50

*Fear not that thy life shall come to an end, but rather fear
that it shall never have a beginning.*

—John Henry Newman

Gospel: Matthew 26:1–27:66

[17] On the first day of Unleavened Bread
the disciples came to Jesus, saying,
"Where do you want us to make the
preparations for you to eat the Passover?"
[18] He said, "Go into the city to a certain
man, and say to him, 'The Teacher says,
My time is near; I will keep the Passover
at your house with my disciples.' "
[19] So the disciples did as Jesus
had directed them, and they
prepared the Passover meal.

MONDAY IN HOLY WEEK

Second Reading: Hebrews 9:11–15

[15] ... he is the mediator of a new covenant, so that those who are called may receive the promised eternal inheritance....

Gospel: John 12:1–11

[1] Six days before the Passover Jesus came to Bethany, the home of Lazarus, whom he had raised from the dead. [2] There they gave a dinner for him. Martha served, and Lazarus was one of those at the table with him. [3] Mary took a pound of costly perfume made of pure nard, anointed Jesus' feet, and wiped them with her hair. The house was filled with the fragrance of the perfume. [4] But Judas Iscariot, one of his disciples (the one who was about to betray him), said, [5] "Why was this perfume not sold for three hundred denarii and the money given to the poor?" [6] (He said this not because he cared about the poor, but because he was a thief; he kept the common purse and used to steal what was put into it.) [7] Jesus said, "Leave her alone. She bought it so that she might keep it for the day of my burial. [8] You always have the poor with you, but you do not always have me."

First Reading: Isaiah 42:1–9

[1] Here is my servant, whom I
uphold,
my chosen, in whom my
soul delights;
I have put my spirit upon
him;
he will bring forth justice
to the nations....
[4] He will not grow faint or
be crushed
until he has established
justice in the earth;
and the coastlands wait for
his teaching.

*Your steadfast love, O LORD, extends to the heavens,
your faithfulness to the clouds.*
— Psalm 36:5

52

TUESDAY IN HOLY WEEK

Gospel: John 12:20–36

32 "... And I, when I am lifted up from the earth, will draw all people to myself." 33 He said this to indicate the kind of death he was to die.

First Reading: Isaiah 49:1–6

6 "... I will give you as a light to the
    nations,
      that my salvation may reach to the end
      of the earth."

Second Reading: 1 Corinthians 1:18–25

18 For the message about the cross is foolishness to those who are perishing, but to us who are being saved it is the power of God. 19 For it is written,
    "I will destroy the wisdom of the wise,
      and the discernment of the discern-
      ing I will thwart."
20 Where is the one who is wise? Where is the scribe? Where is the debater of this age? Has not God made foolish the wisdom of the world? 21 For since, in the wisdom of God, the world did not know God through wisdom, God decided, through the foolishness of our proclamation, to save those who believe.

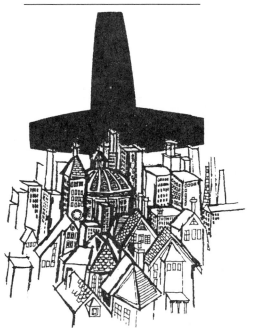

O God, do not be far from me;
*   O my God, make haste to help me!*
*   — Psalm 71:12*

WEDNESDAY IN
HOLY WEEK

First Reading: Isaiah 50:4–9a

⁵ The Lord GOD has opened my ear,
    and I was not rebellious,
    I did not turn backward.
⁶ I gave my back to those who struck me,
    and my cheeks to those who pulled out
        the beard;
I did not hide my face
    from shame and spitting.

Second Reading: Romans 5:6–11

⁶ For while we were still weak, at the
right time Christ died for the ungodly.
⁷ Indeed, rarely will anyone die for a
righteous person — though perhaps for
a good person someone might actually
dare to die. ⁸ But God proves his love
for us in that while we were still sinners
Christ died for us. ⁹ Much more surely
then, now that we have been justified by
his blood, will we be saved through him
from the wrath of God. ¹⁰ For if while we
were enemies, we were reconciled to God
through the death of his Son, much more
surely, having been reconciled, will we be
saved by his life. ¹¹ But more than that,
we even boast in God through our Lord
Jesus Christ, through whom we have now
received reconciliation.

Sometimes our light goes out but it is blown again into flame by an encounter with another human being. Each of us owes deepest thanks to those who have rekindled this inner light.

— **Albert Schweitzer**

Gospel: Matthew 26:14–25

---

[14] Then one of the twelve, who was called Judas Iscariot, went to the chief priests [15] and said, "What will you give me if I betray him to you?" They paid him thirty pieces of silver. [16] And from that time on he began to look for an opportunity to betray him....

[20] When it was evening, he took his place with the twelve; [21] and while they were eating, he said, "Truly I tell you, one of you will betray me." [22] And they became greatly distressed and began to say to him one after another, "Surely not I, Lord?" [23] He answered, "The one who has dipped his hand into the bowl with me will betray me. [24] The Son of Man goes as it is written of him, but woe to that one by whom the Son of Man is betrayed! It would have been better for that one not to have been born." [25] Judas, who betrayed him, said, "Surely not I, Rabbi?" He replied, "You have said so."

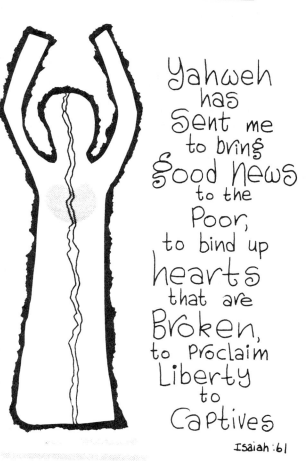

Yahweh has Sent me to bring Good news to the Poor, to bind up hearts that are Broken, to Proclaim Liberty to Captives

Isaiah :61

The Lord God helps me . . .

I wish that they could realize that they are wasting their time. A bishop will die, but the church of God — the people — will never die.

–Archbishop Oscar Romero

MAUNDY THURSDAY

Invitation for Commitment

Come, Come!

Come and celebrate
   the supper of the Lord.
Let's make an enormous loaf
   of bread,
let's bring abundant wine,
like in the wedding at Cana.

Women, don't forget the salt.
Men, bring along the yeast.
Come, guests.
Come, many quests!
You who are lame, blind,
   crippled, poor.

Come quickly!
Let's follow the recipe our Lord
   gave us.
All of us,
let's knead the dough together
with our hands.
See how the bread rises,
Watch with joy.

For today we celebrate
a meeting with our Lord.
Today we renew
our commitment to the
Kingdom.
Nobody should go hungry
   any more.

          –Elsa Tamez

First Reading: Exodus 12:1–14

^{12} . . . on all the gods of Egypt I will execute judgments: I am the LORD. ^{13} The blood shall be a sign for you on the houses where you live: when I see the blood, I will pass over you, and no plague shall destroy you when I strike the land of Egypt. ^{14} This day shall be a day of remembrance for you. You shall celebrate it as a festival to the LORD; throughout your generations you shall observe it as a perpetual ordinance.

Second Reading: 1 Corinthians 11:17–32

^{23} For I received from the Lord what I also handed on to you, that the Lord Jesus on the night when he was betrayed took a loaf of bread, ^{24} and when he had given thanks, he broke it and said, "This is my body that is for you. Do this in remembrance of me." ^{25} In the same way he took the cup also, after supper, saying, "This cup is the new covenant in my blood. Do this, as often as you drink it, in remembrance of me." ^{26} For as often as you eat this bread and drink the cup, you proclaim the Lord's death until he comes.
^{27} Whoever, therefore, eats the bread or drinks the cup of the Lord in an unworthy manner will be answerable for the body and blood of the Lord. ^{28} Examine yourselves, and only then eat of the bread and drink of the cup.

There is no such thing as my bread. All bread is ours and is given to me. To others through me and to me through others.

— Meister Eckhart

Gospel: John 13:1–17, 34

[2] ... And during supper [3] Jesus, knowing that the Father had given all things into his hands, and that he had come from God and was going to God, [4] got up from the table, took off his outer robe, and tied a towel around himself. [5] Then he poured water into a basin and began to wash the disciples' feet and to wipe them with the towel that was tied around him....

[12] After he had washed their feet, had put on his robe, and had returned to the table, he said to them, "Do you know what I have done to you? [13] You call me Teacher and Lord — and you are right, for that is what I am. [14] So if I, your Lord and Teacher, have washed your feet, you also ought to wash one another's feet...."

[34] "I give you a new commandment, that you love one another. Just as I have loved you, you also should love one another."

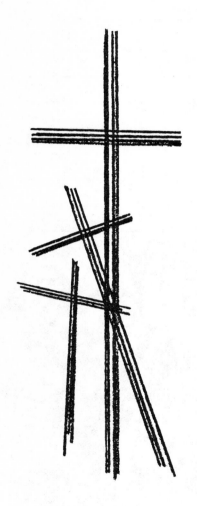

First Reading: Isaiah 52:13–53:12

[3] He was despised and rejected by others;
    a man of suffering and acquainted with
      infirmity;
and as one from whom others hide their
    faces
    he was despised, and we held him of
      no account.
[4] Surely he has borne our infirmities
    and carried our diseases;
yet we accounted him stricken,
    struck down by God, and afflicted.

Second Reading: Hebrews 4:14–16, 5:7–9

[14] Since, then, we have a great high priest
who has passed through the heavens,
Jesus, the Son of God, let us hold fast to
our confession. [15] For we do not have a
high priest who is unable to sympathize
with our weaknesses, but we have one who
in every respect has been tested as we are,
yet without sin. [16] Let us therefore ap-
proach the throne of grace with boldness,
so that we may receive mercy and find
grace to help in time of need.

When Jesus...confides in us that he is "acquainted with Grief," we listen, for that is also Acquaintance of our Own.

— Emily Dickinson

Gospel: John 18:1–19:42

[16] Then he handed him over to them to be crucified.

So they took Jesus; [17] and carrying the cross by himself, he went out to what is called The Place of the Skull, which in Hebrew is called Golgotha. [18] There they crucified him, and with him two others, one on either side, with Jesus between them. [19] Pilate also had an inscription written and put on the cross. It read, "Jesus of Nazareth, the King of the Jews."

He has borne our infirmities . . .

Christian faith is neither neutral nor indifferent to what is happening to our land. Jesus says clearly, "I am come to heal the brokenhearted." He is "the man of sorrows and acquainted with grief." He does not only come to heal those who are broken, but he himself experiences it, he himself is the object of repression and death by those who are opposed to life itself. The Gospel stands on the side of those who are broken for justice's sake, that is, on the side of the people who are crying out for justice to attain an elementary level of life and who are being obstructed in their progress towards it.

–Ecumenical Movement for Human Rights

59

RESURRECCIÓN

First Reading: Lamentations 3:37–58

⁴⁶ All our enemies
    have opened their mouths against us;
⁴⁷ panic and pitfall have come upon us,
    devastation and destruction.
⁴⁸ My eyes flow with rivers of tears
    because of the destruction of my
        people.
⁴⁹ My eyes will flow without ceasing,
    without respite,
⁵⁰ until the LORD from heaven
    looks down and sees.
⁵¹ My eyes cause me grief
    at the fate of all the young women in
        my city....
⁵⁵ I called on your name, O LORD,
    from the depths of the pit;
⁵⁶ you heard my plea, "Do not close your ear
    to my cry for help, but give me relief!"
⁵⁷ You came near when I called on you;
    you said, "Do not fear!"
⁵⁸ You have taken up my cause, O LORD,
    you have redeemed my life.

Second Reading: Hebrews 4:1–16

¹² Indeed, the word of God is living and
active, sharper than any two-edged sword,
piercing until it divides soul from spirit,
joints from marrow; it is able to judge
the thoughts and intentions of the heart.
¹³ And before him no creature is hidden,
but all are naked and laid bare to the eyes
of the one to whom we must render an
account.

...all dimensions of life are revelatory of God — nature, our relationships, the joys, sorrows, conflicts, and celebrations that shape the dailiness of our individual lives, and the larger social, political, and economic realities of our time.
— Maria Riley, O.P.

Third Reading: Romans 8:1–11

[11] If the Spirit of him who raised Jesus from the dead dwells in you, he who raised Christ from the dead will give life to your mortal bodies also through his Spirit that dwells in you.

. . . when heaven is wedded to earth . . .

This is the night
when Christians everywhere,
washed clean of sin
and freed from all defilement,
are restored to grace
and grow together in holiness.
This is the night when Jesus Christ
broke the chains of death
and rose triumphant from the grave.
The power of this holy night
dispels all evil,
washes guilt away,
restores lost innocence,
brings mourners joy.
Night truly blessed
when heaven is wedded to earth
and God to us.
May the Morning Star which never sets
find this flame still burning:
Christ, that Morning Star,
who came back from the dead,
and shed his peaceful light
on all humankind.
—"Exultet" from Easter Vigil,
Roman Liturgy (adapted)

EASTER

EASTER SUNDAY

First Reading: Acts 10:34–43

[34] Then Peter began to speak to them:
"I truly understand that God shows no
partiality, [35] but in every nation anyone
who fears him and does what is right
is acceptable to him. [36] You know the
message he sent to the people of Israel,
preaching peace by Jesus Christ — he
is Lord of all. [37] That message spread
throughout Judea, beginning in Galilee
after the baptism that John announced:
[38] how God anointed Jesus of Nazareth
with the Holy Spirit and with power; how
he went about doing good and healing
all who were oppressed by the devil, for
God was with him. [39] We are witnesses
to all that he did both in Judea and in
Jerusalem. They put him to death by
hanging him on a tree; [40] but God raised
him on the third day....

Second Reading: Colossians 3:1–4

[1] So if you have been raised with Christ,
seek the things that are above, where
Christ is, seated at the right hand of God.
[2] Set your minds on things that are above,
not on things that are on earth, [3] for you
have died, and your life is hidden with
Christ in God. [4] When Christ who is
your life is revealed, then you also will
be revealed with him in glory.

May the God who shakes heaven and earth, whom death could not contain, who lives to disturb and heal us, bless you with power to go forth and proclaim the gospel. Amen.

— Janet Morley

Gospel: John 20:1–9 (10–18)

[1] Early on the first day of the week, while it was still dark, Mary Magdalene came to the tomb and saw that the stone had been removed from the tomb. [2] So she ran and went to Simon Peter and the other disciple, the one whom Jesus loved, and said to them, "They have taken the Lord out of the tomb, and we do not know where they have laid him." [3] Then Peter and the other disciple set out and went toward the tomb. [4] The two were running together, but the other disciple outran Peter and reached the tomb first. [5] He bent down to look in and saw the linen wrappings lying there, but did not go in. [6] Then Simon Peter came, following him, and went into the tomb. He saw the linen wrappings lying there, [7] and the cloth that had been on Jesus' head, not lying with the linen wrappings but rolled up in a place by itself. [8] Then the other disciple, who reached the tomb first, also went in, and he saw and believed; [9] for as yet they did not understand the scripture, that he must rise from the dead. [10] Then the disciples returned to their homes.

I believe

I believe in God,
  who is love
  and who has given the earth
  to all people.
I believe in Jesus Christ,
  who came to heal us,
  and to free us
  from all forms of oppression.
I believe in the Spirit of God
  who works in and through all
  who have turned towards
    the truth.
I believe in the community of
    faith
  which is called to be
  at the service of all people.
I believe in God's promise
  to finally destroy
  the power of sin in us all,
  and to establish the kingdom
  of justice and peace
  to all humankind.

*–An Indonesian creed,
Christian Conference of Asia*

ACKNOWLEDGMENTS

The following sources for passages used in *This Fast I Choose* are gratefully acknowledged:

With All God's People: The New Ecumenical Prayer Cycle, compiled by John Carden (Geneva: WCC Publications, 1989; Mystic, Conn.: Twenty-Third Publications, 1990), is a rich source of prayers and statements of faith from Christians and churches around the world. The following are included in this volume: Prayer from Nigeria (p. 8); a Melanesian islander's prayer (p. 11); Congolese hymn (p. 21); a prayer from Sri Lanka (p. 24); prayer from Pakistan (p. 27); prayer by Toyohiko Kagawa (p. 29); "Sharing the same bread" (p. 31); "O God of the ever present crosses" (p. 39); prayer of an African Christian (p. 46); tenth-century African hymn (p. 50); an Indonesian creed (p. 63).

Credo from the Mass of the Marginalized People (p. 43) is found in *Confessing Our Faith around the World, III: The Caribbean and Central America*, ed. Hans-Georg Link (Geneva: World Council of Churches, 1984); "I believe, but increase my faith" (p. 19), "Manifesto to the Nation" (p. 25), and the statement from the Ecumenical Movement for Human Rights, Buenos Aires (p. 59) are included in *Confessing Our Faith around the World, IV: South America*, ed. Hans-Georg Link (Geneva: World Council of Churches, 1985).

"I am no longer afraid of death" (p. 35), by Julia Esquivel, is published in *Churches in Solidarity with Women: Prayers and poems, songs and stories* (Geneva: WCC Publications, 1988), p. 19, and is used here with permission of the author.

"Invitation for Commitment" (p. 56), by Elsa Tamez, is included in *Jesus Christ the Life of the World*, a worship book for the Sixth Assembly of the World Council of Churches (Geneva, 1983); it is used here with permission of the author.

The following sources for illustrations used in *This Fast I Choose* are also gratefully acknowledged:

Pages 5, 18, 23, 26, 55: Eunice Cudzewicz, Medical Mission Sisters, Philadelphia, PA 19111. Designed for the Office on Global Education, National Council of Churches, 2115 N. Charles St., Baltimore, MD 21218. Used with permission.

Pages 14, 29, 33, 49: Mechtilt; p. 21: "Mother," by Hong Song Dam; p. 40: from *In God's Image*, Singapore; p. 45: Tomiyama Taeko; p. 57: "Last Supper," by Sadao Watanabe; p. 62: Coralie Ling. All reproduced from *Ecumenical Decade 1988–1998, Churches in Solidarity with Women: Prayers and poems, songs and stories* (Geneva: WCC Publications, 1988).

Page 16: Meinrad Craighead, "Noah's Ark," from *Liturgical Art*, Sheed & Ward, Box 414492, Kansas City, MO, 64141. Used with permission.

Pages 17, 30: *Graphics for Sunday: Illustrations for the Church's Year, Cycles A, B, and C*, by Susan Daily I.B.V.M. (Burwood, Vic., Australia: Collins Dove, 1987).

Page 34: "The Labor Cross," by Fritz Eichenberg, 1954, wood engraving from a portfolio of illustrations, published in the *Catholic Worker*, 1949–1982. Collection of Mark Solomon. Used with permission.

Page 38: NETWORK, National Catholic Social Justice Lobby, Washington, D.C.

Page 60: Sr. Helen David Brancato, I.H.M. Reproduced from *Focus on Central America*, Maryknoll Missioners, Maryknoll, NY 10545.

Every effort has been made to acknowledge the original sources for the material used here; if we have unknowingly infringed on any copyright, we apologize and will make the appropriate corrections in future printings.

All Scripture passages are quoted from the New Revised Standard Version. The licensed English-language publishers of this translation are Cambridge University Press, Holman Bible Publishers, Thomas Nelson Publishers, Oxford University Press, World Bible Publishers, and Zondervan Publishers.